LANDMASS

AND OTHER POEMS

Published by Dreaming Deer Press
Marietta, GA, USA 30067

ISBN-13: 978-0615949284
ISBN-10: 0615949282

Cover art by Joseph S. Plum, watercolor & ink, 1970.

Printed in the United States of America

For poetry books, CDs & DVDs
by Joseph S. Plum, please visit:

www.JoePlum.com

LandMass

and other poems

Joseph S. Plum

Dreaming Deer Press

Preface

    The poems written in this book were transcribed from the original oral poetry that was crafted in the bardic tradition of dreaming and living a lifetime in connection with nature. The hope is that by writing down the poems and collecting them into books, they may travel widely and be shared with the world. If you have a chance, please say these poems aloud. In this way, the beauty and power of traditional bardic poetry will live on through your voice.

Artist's Statement

no matter

how strong

the anchor

or how large

the sail,

someday

a greater wind

will prevail.

-Joseph Samuel Plum

Contents

for the offspring

"is it sweet

or is it sour?

is it weakness

or is it power?

is it fruit

or is it flower?

alive

in the moment

not the hour."

paradigm creed

do you believe in seeds
planted in wild places,
in the taste of river mist
and the smell of sages?
do you believe in mountains
while crossing the borderline
and bridges in the desert
spanning the depths of time?
do you believe in the journey of a soul,
in destinations made manifest
by the dreams and visions that we hold?
do you believe in a spirit life
fashioned by design
stretching across a threshold
created by leaving autonomy behind?
do you believe in sunlight
filtering through green leaves
and in the shadows of untold winters
hugging the branches of trees?
yes, there is a pathway
extending from this moment at hand

enduring throughout eternity

in the heart and breath of man.

   do you believe in an open gate

and radiant splendor,

in engagements ongoing

which struggle to surrender

meaning to solitude

and the ability to engender

space without time

empowered

with the impulse to remember

human beings as children

and pure light

as the great defender

of a faith that is defined

until finally freed

by a mind which accepts

then releases the paradigm creed?

tell me,
please tell me,
do you believe?
do you believe in seeds
planted in wild places?

comes a moment

listen.
our language encircles us
with prisms of knowledge
that break clear light
into pyramids of color
and threads of darkness.
by the hand of our faith,
together with truth,
these words are woven into lies
on the loom of desire
until we are wrapped
in a silk of unbroken reflections
against which our fresh
and untried wings
push!

in a wordless way
rain washes dust
from ten thousand days,
while in evening's deep
and dreamless cool,

crickets dance and drink

from morning's crystal dew.

black red wing birds

and flutter bys,

thunder poems

sung in dragonfly,

dusty fingers stalk the moon

to trace a pillowed sky

as a setting sun of ashen hue

tells this world good bye.

up from across a sea of satin breeze

ageless anthems roll,

misleading those who would be led,

overturning my empty bowl.

   yes, i have no faith

in firm belief,

said the night mist to the wind.

in passing over

the depths of winter's sky,

the stars of spring shine in.

yes, i have no faith

in winter's spring

or in summer's sudden fall.

just on the grounds

of what is see,

i have no faith at all.

and yet against the skies

of what i feel

my eternal spirit sails,

bringing back to me

a fuller life

of a faith that never fails.

   in the twilight

just beginning

there is an instant,

never ending,

when we go off

and spinning

out across the milky way.

in the darkness

always turning

towards the light

of another morning

comes a moment

without warning

when we're finally

on our way.

   in the ages

that are fast approaching

there are those

who awake unknowing,

on a journey

from which they

can never stray.

while here

in this dim light of evening

i lie half asleep,

rocking

in the cradle of another day.

   yes,

there are no words

to the tune

that my grandfather's

mother's humming,

while to the beat

beneath my legs,

someone else's

feet are running

towards a field

of far off stars

to where

Orion's child is coming.

yes, winter's

eastern sky at night

sends home to earth

man's delight.

on heavenly wings

of ancestral light,

Orion's child is coming.

   elsewhere

is Orion's child,

in whose heart

the hunters' pulse

is pounding,

beating out a rhythm

of ten thousand years

in every newborn's cry

resounding

with a fullness

which draws us near

to the center

of a universe

that's expanding,

until in the silence

left behind

we arrive

at a better understanding

of who and where

and what we are,

and why the creator

is not demanding

that we take our position

among those stars

and reach out

for the hand

that's extending.

   yes, elsewhere

is this god of mine,

at the speed of light

reclining,

at rest

on a sea of sighs,

in each breath

deciding

whether or not

to be here

among us now,

where that moment

of departure

is always

almost arriving.

ice

    water

    ice

    is an endless flow.

       ice

    water

    ice

    is forever more.

       yes we are

    ice water ice

    until we are

    just once more,

    ice.

the frozen lands

in these hands
there sleeps a musician
whose instrument
has never been made,
a composer of songs
which will not be played,
the keeper of melody
whose harmonies are being saved
for a performance of release
from the shallows of an earthly grave.
in this heart there is a fire
whose spark shall remain
even after being swallowed
by the confines of that eternal flame,
and where the ashes are each spread
long after the warmth has all fled,
in the air there is a voice
which will rise up
and breathe life into words
that have never before been said.
yes, there is a dispeller of night

in this world of the spiritually dead,

a bringer of sunlight

to these frozen lands

whose ice once fed

springs that would turn to rivers,

to wash away dark blindness

from these eyes in our heads,

tears to mirror dreams of great price,

asleep in our beds.

    in this life

many a time we have acted

like children of the material gods,

those who by thinking

thought they could conquer

the unbeatable odds.

we have been youthful spirits

with no clan to protect or profess,

we have been infants without angels

who would guard us and then bless.

    although we are bound

to the body,

still we have eyes

that gaze skyward.

so by searching the heavens

with no thought for reward

while keeping an ear to this earth,

an enchanting duet

of musical debate can be heard.

for what the gods in their wisdom

proclaim as being absolute,

my great mother in her laughter

calls absurd.

"the doorway

to mystery

opens

with a combination

lock.

unseen

the ceiling

of the sky only

overshadows

the planking

of our

heart. "

-*Aerion Cenote*

LandMass

prologue

Arrival

I found myself walking in a dream through an ancient city. Suddenly, I awoke to the reality of the dream; knowing that I was dreaming and at the same instant asleep in my bed. The memory of both worlds at my fingertips. As I was walking, my attention was drawn to a stairway winding up the outside of a large stone building. Climbing the steps, I came to a small, arched door four or five stories up. The building was a cathedral.

Passing through the doorway, I found myself on a narrow stone ledge, inside, looking down at a distant tile floor which held a mosaic pattern. Opposite was another small door. Crossing over, I stepped outside onto the upper reaches of a red tile roof. It was very steep.

Carefully, I made my way down to the very edge of this roof. Hanging on with my toes and my fingertips, I looked over the edge. Far below, I could see ocean waves crashing against very large stones. The wind was blowing. Looking deep into the wild ocean surf, a thought came to me.

"No one knows how death begins. Maybe death begins when you believe that you are dreaming."

Then I thought, "Now is a chance to find out. Why don't you just jump?"

So I jumped.

I hit the water and the rocks hard, and it hurt. I was cut into many, many little pieces.

My momentum carried me through the rocks and the waves, on down into the earth itself, until I found myself again assembled, standing upright in a tunnel beneath the sea. As I stood there looking down the passageway, I could see a young man dressed in white. He turned to the right and disappeared.

I walked to the end of that passage and, turning to the right, I could see him ahead of me once more. Again, he turned to the right and disappeared. This went on for some time. Finally, I came upon him in a room with a sunken floor and a railing carved entirely out of brown stone.

A soft, translucent light from thin arched windows flooded the room. The young man, glowing white, sat upon a long, low table.

I walked up to the man, all the while knowing that I was dreaming. He had straight black hair and was very pale. We talked for awhile. He told me that, in our waking world, he was lying in a hospital bed, dying. And when he was unconscious to the waking world, he would appear in this dreaming world we were sharing. He said that this process had been going on for some time, and that when he was conscious there in the hospital, he was not here. He was beginning to spend more and more time in the passageways under the cathedral.

At one point we clasped hands, and I helped him stand up from the table. As he stood, I saw that there were words embossed in gold upon the table, which was burgundy in color. The words said, "LandMass Poetry."

It was then that I realized I was looking at a book, a very large book! Together we opened the book, somehow pinching the first few pages between the cover and our fingers. The first word that I read was "If." A great big "I" with green vines and pale flowers intertwined around it, then a small "f" after.

Together we read the book until suddenly I was overcome by a feeling telling me to read no further. Closing the book, I found myself awake once more in my cabin. The fire was out and I was cold. This is how landmass poetry came into this world.

Perhaps in some not-too-distant future, I will once more travel those passageways. And like that young man, I will begin to be there more and more. I will open the book and read on, but for now…

landmass

if you swing

a sword

at the head

of any man,

dagger-like,

the handle

will cut

your hand.

if the force

of the blow

you would contain,

the tip

of the tongue

of the blade

will sing

your name.

then if

you should

cry out loud,

mummified vitality

will become

a shroud

until with

spirit eyes

and heart

wide open,

wisdom

is conveyed

through

the ancient gift

of thoughts

unspoken.

    when growth

begins

towards the sun

a pathway

of light

has just begun,

when shadows

and blindness

are sliced

away

the thrust

to live

leads into

a brighter day.

    then when

your sword

of might

cuts

nothing more

than circles

in the air,

holographic contrails

of shimmering reality

will appear

shining

like eyes

of a ghost

looking through

a living mirror,

hoping

that somehow

heartfelt attention

can repair

mindful rips

in the upper atmosphere,

until from

beyond the grace

of heavens

a storm cloud

of ancient relatives

suddenly appears

raining down

upon us

with unearthly care,

flooding away

every unfounded

fear,

washing out

from the mind

that blank

hypnotic stare,

leaving behind

nothing

nothing

except these eyes

that shine

but just can

no longer glare!

at the back
of the night wind
they say
there is
a far away country,
a region
where shores
are beyond
the reach
of pain,
a place
where sleep
comes easy
from days
filled with living
not ever needing
a dark time
of acting insane.
in our hearts
i know
there is a homeland,
a world

where good fortune
and feeling
remain the same,
a landscape
grown
out of hunger
for love
that requires
neither glory
or shame.
    in the mind's eye
there is a distance
beyond recovery,
a journey
of insight
not easy
to explain,
a quest
of internal illumination,
one that begins
with no thought
for title
or fame.

in this life

(right now)

there can be

a moment

of awakening,

the miracle

of many worlds

sharing one sky,

an impulsive reaction

to instinctive wisdom

which knows

without ever

asking why.

through your breath

there flows

a power

to draw down

heaven

from the farthest reaches

of deepest space,

lifting up from within us

the hollow center

of a swirling vortex

of solitary grace.

    behind this dream

(right now)

there lives another

asleep,

yet, somehow

keeping pace,

granting a rhythm

for all the runners

who never began

but must now

finish

this human race.

    if we are

to live

in a world

without borders,

first there must be

freedom

from the culturally

indoctrinated state,

creating a country

whose capital concept

is kindness.

listen

carefully

to the needs

of others,

become

an open doorway,

do not discriminate.

    then

when the old speech

comes on the tongue

and desire

flames up

in the blood,

when the wind

cries

the stars

out each night,

longing after

the souls

who have left

this world unloved,

then

unsettled destiny

shall walk about

with a lantern

of dream light

cradled

in each hand,

looking

to give

vision reserved

for those

who sleep

with half-closed eyes,

that someday

we might awake

then struggle

to understand

that there

is no poverty

in darkness.

a dream

of fishes

revolving

around the sun,

an eclectic expression

of unspoken devotion

conceived

with innocence

when this moment

and eternity

were one.

    yes, there is

no need

for continued

development

now

that the pendulum

of time

has swung.

    all that's required

is child-like

desire,

each of us

believing

that our own

vision

of tomorrow

has finally come.

    for what does

the stem

know

of root

or flower

if not for

a hollowness within,

and what does

one instant

know

of a journey

of hours

if not for

the season

in which to begin?

    here

are the places

waiting

for footfalls,

here

is a remedy

to original sin.

here

is an echo

leading

through listening

into the temples

that wait

in emptiness

until they quake

with resonance,

throbbing breathless

just beneath

our skin.

heavy

with feeling,

scented

by dreaming,

after

the days

in far away

places,

we shed

memories

like well-loved

clothing

whose need

is now absent,

time

outgrown.

    put them

in keeping,

fresh

from the folding,

alongside

the tears

waiting

for faces,

into

those eyes

well known

for opening

in a flash

of remembrance

yet to come.

    awake

to the morning

of a journey

just dawning,

breathe

in today

through

limitless spaces,

dress now

in newness

as is

our promise,

hearts are so small

and birthing

must go on.

    fresh

from an ocean

of everyday living,

with the current

just returning

into the dark air,

raises

a quick moving

wonder,

stream-lined

energy bundle,

great god-child
of the sun!
    embedded
in growing,
diminished
by knowing,
the upstream
swimmer
dispenses graces,
full into
the future flowing,
cryptic jewel,
radiant hum.
    storms arise
on the ocean,
    clouds move
inland from sea,
with the electric
hand of lightning
the ancients
are searching
my dreams
to be free.

up and down

the shore line

　　in and out

the coast,

weaving

among the watchful

with all the airs

of an ancestral ghost,

　　they move into

a mortal body,

they look outward

with glowing eyes,

they grab

any heart

between their hands,

crushing

all dreams

with their sighs.

　　around their necks

are hammered pendants,

living slivers

of a silver moon.

at each breast

there clings

a human being,

bodies bent

into a cryptic rune.

first there are

the women fair,

stardust strands

glittering

make up

their hair,

fingers

bent gentle

in repose

give

a healing touch

to those

in the flow.

    then comes

the man-child,

dark and wild,

fiercely

crying softly

all the while.

together

we travel,

never having

rest,

each breath

drawn

sharpens

a mirrored

silhouette.

the ancient

primal minds

are the mountains

scattered

across this earth.

for them,

each thought

is a pathway tunnel.

for us,

a passage

of rebirth.

when the sun

no longer

comes up

with the morning

to set again

in the west,

when every movement

is a turning moment

inviting reunion

through communion

with the collective

primal breath,

    then

from beneath

the seas

of dark foreboding

from within

the oceans

of life's

discontent,

there will arise

out of every horizon

a vision

to put

all our senses
to the test.

    in the deepening
quick remembrance
where each
indwelling impulse
falls
into step,
there through
the awakening instant,
the prime creator
responds
by giving
every future
a dim
and distant
dream-like
past.

    struck hard,
the drum head
quivers

up the hand
of man,
a dying vibration
delivers
a new sense
out of nowhere,
who in nakedness
shivers,
waiting now
as the gift
is unwrapped
from the givers.

    in the house
of god
his children
are restless.
on the holy mountain
the temple valley
is leaning,
while from
the grave mound
of future generations

into this world

spirits are bleeding,

weaving

a blood trail

of uneasy feeling

into the fabric

of everyday living.

    through the sky

first light

is still falling,

striking

the eye

with the hope

of recalling

a promise

whose workings

open

into the center

of a being

whose finest thoughts

are like

birds in the sky,

turning

and wheeling,

arising

in unison

yet conceived apart.

    a pathway

of liberation

leading directly

through migration

into a fire beacon

burning

in the heart.

forever

    each seeker's

destiny

    is always

individually

    the same.

flutter

    to the light.

fall

    to the flame.

flame holders,

fire feeders,

smoke tenders,

tributaries

of glowing light

burn bright

without consuming

long dead

empty night.

bed of eons,

warm river rising,

epic journeys

flow in our heart.

wooden souls

of stick people

rub together

to touch

in tribute

until torched

before the idol

of eternal spark.

treasure mound

of ancient duty,

grace
of ancestors,
love cry
devoid
of flash
must now forever,
in undisputed
fallen glory,
from the wind
guard
this house
of ash.
      oath of dust
just returning
cast no shadow
to the ground,
beyond limits
set by understanding
a still voice
approaches sound.
cross these hills,
a fierce allegiance
hung

with ribbons cold

brings for us

a map

to heaven

on which

starry dreams

unfold.

    treasure guard

armed

with silver,

ancient ways

fixed in gold,

restless flesh

bent

on concealing

leads

in hunger

to a goal.

    here are steps

obtained

from children,

eyes

to surrender

in consideration
of the whole,
scattered lives
to be remembered
by the consolidation
of a soul.
    precious seed
locked
in beginning,
sing
upon the wave.
anthems quick
in begetting,
followers
for the brave.
    to know
no time
in active measure
is the one
sure secret
all great things
must truly hold,
like a face

never fading

from daily favor,

this moment

is a gift

of forever

and should

be treated

with all respect

due any inherited

treasure trove.

    heart

of beauty beating,

breath

of vapor clean,

when will

being together

leave us

waking

in a dream?

    water

fallen cold

turns tears

to ice

from inside,

fire

gone back

to ash

draws flame

from lighted eyes.

sleeping

in the etheric

overlap,

waiting out

the complex collapse,

watching

as the eons pass,

the constructive soul

cannot help

but surpass

what each mind

leaves behind

in any attempt

to grasp

what reason

will define

as time

in the face

of death,

where fear

becomes a mask

to hide behind

and survive

until our loved ones

no longer ask

for these feelings

that we lack.

    thin line

of feeling,

knife edge

that cuts

both sides

of the barrier

meeting,

now that enough

is enough,

watershed

of meaning

held open

like a readied cup,

deep well
of believing
never filling up,
mute hand
extended
sped away
from me,
swiftly
dies a river
swallowed
by the sea.
     storms arise
on the ocean,
clouds move inland
from the sea
with the electric
hand of lightning,
very soon
the ancients
will be searching
your dreams
to be free.

for today

leads

into tomorrow

and draws us

very near.

rest

with ease

in wonder,

the house

of love

has no room

for fear!

"…there

is a secret

i shall

always keep

until there is no one

to keep it from.

for i have

a message

i shall never speak

until long after

i've lost this tongue.

i know

another voice,

somewhere,

will rise up beneath

a setting sun

to give this earth

its closing prayer

in a language

and a scripture

from a time

yet to come…"

-from language of birds

About the Author

Joseph Samuel Plum is a direct descendant of Welsh bards and Native American spirit. He lives in South Central Iowa within a group of trees where he composes and presents oral bardic poetry of original nature. He has been doing this for fifty years. This is his third book.

Books by Joseph S. Plum

RELICS

CONCENTRIC DEVOTION

LANDMASS AND OTHER POEMS

BOOK OF SHADOWS

HUMAN LANDSCAPE

OLD PATH

NOBLE REMNANTS

GATHERING POEMS

www.JoePlum.com

www.ingramcontent.com/pod-product-compliance
Lightning Source LLC
LaVergne TN
LVHW021546080426
835509LV00019B/2862